Story of building tomorrow's generation

Md Bayazid Khan

ISBN 978-93-5610-074-9

Published in India 2022 by Pencil

Contributors:
Co-Author: Mrs. Nahid Parvin

A brand of
One Point Six Technologies Pvt. Ltd.
123, Building J2, Shram Seva Premises,
Wadala Truck Terminal, Wadala (E)
Mumbai 400037, Maharashtra, INDIA
E connect@thepencilapp.com
W www.thepencilapp.com

Author biography

Author of the book, Md Bayazid Khan was born on June 15, 1967 in the district of Cumilla. His father, Md Harunur Rashid Khan was a service holder who died in 2017 and his mother, Payara Begum is a housewife. He is master degree holder in Economics. He has been working in the primary education sector in Bangladesh since 1997. He has experiences of working as Upazila Education Officer, Assistant District Primary Education Officer and District Primary Education Officer. He visited United Kingdom and Malaysia to receive training on primary education management, school management, facilitation of training, material development etc. His wife also has been working for primary education sector since 1996 and has experiences of working as Assistant Upazila Education Officer & Upazila Education Officer. Both they have a good reputation for working honestly and with commitment. They have a son, Mohammad Areeb Sharar of fourteen years old. The author has been writing articles for the renowned national English dailies on education and development issues of Bangladesh since 2012.

CONTENTS

Story of building tomorrow's generation

Mr. Khan joined the primary education sector in 1997 as a field level education manager in a remote area of Bangladesh with massive expectation of bringing a visible positive change in this sector. Coming out from the university he, the fresh blooded young energetic guy was pragmatic, confident and optimistic to improve the learning level of primary school children working with commitment and integrity. He had the vision of bringing a huge number of never enrolled and drop out children under basic education dispelling all obstacles. He was also optimistic to improve the teaching-learning process at schools creating a joyful and child-friendly atmosphere. At the outset of his journey in primary education, he confronted undesired impediments on the way of fulfilling his vision. He found a considerable number of never enrolled and drop out children in the hard-to-reach areas, hilly areas, low lying marsh lands, ethnic minority inhabited areas and urban slums. He witnessed poor performances in learning of significant number of students, absence of joyful and participatory teaching-learning process at class rooms, increased rate of absentee students, poor quality physical facilities at schools, meager contact hour, and excessive number of students from poverty stricken families who didn't taking part classroom activities with attention due to victim of malnutrition. He observed absence of teachers' integrity regarding performing duties sincerely and no involvement of parents & stakeholders to academic and infrastructural development at schools. He realized deeply that this is the right area for him to work with dedication and commitment. Knowing, enquiring, analyzing and evaluating data and information regarding the status of basic or elementary education in developing and underdeveloped countries of South Asia, Africa, South & North American countries, Mr. Khan finds a similar scenario.

Mr. Khan predicts that tomorrow's world will be more competitive to survive. So, tomorrow's generation needs to be nourished and developed with skill-based learning so that they may become worthy of skilled workforces compatible to 21st century's labour market demand. Leaving a considerable number of youths uneducated and unskilled, aforesaid nations can never think of improving the economy and even can't save them from confronting all sorts of environmental, cultural and social hazards. He knows that if he can identify the ways of addressing the issues towards ensuring inclusive and skill-based basic education in Bangladesh, it may help other countries too to address the challenges.

Schools are more comfortable for children rather than home. They feel school as a joyful place of playing and enjoying. Realizing the importance of schools on children's learning, Mr. Khan presented a proposal to

higher authority for making each and every primary school child and learning friendly to learners.

To make effective primary school

Primary schools have a pivotal role in developing a solid foundation of primary education among students. The purposes of primary schools are not only to learn academic contents but also to develop children physically, intellectually, morally, emotionally, socially and aesthetically. Children definitely should have development in these areas in early stages in their life to become good human beings. And primary schools are the only places of rearing and nourishing children to achieve the purposes of primary school as schools are the first formal institution of children outside the family environment. But parents are facing problems now-a-days in selecting primary schools to get their offspring admitted due to the lack of a sufficient number of reputed good schools.

The quality of primary schools has always been of interest to the discerning parents. Parents often talk to others about the merits of primary schools, particularly at those crucial times when their offspring are about to start formal education. Parents firmly believe that primary schools are the only place of developing mastery of fundamentals of education among their children. So they have a tendency to select reputed primary schools for their children, and parents always wrongly differentiate between a good school and a bad school by comparing only examination results although there are so many factors for judging the quality of a school. Due to brilliant academic results in the examinations parents have the tendency to get their kids admitted to the limited number of reputed primary schools at headquarters. As a result, reputed schools are compelled to admit a huge number of students beyond their capacity. Students of these schools are coming from different school catchments areas and most of them are from socially advantaged families. Since parents have the intention to get admission of their offspring to these good schools by any means, the schools are overloaded by students and therefore the quality of teaching-learning activities falls.

On the other hand a huge number of students drop out of schools during the five-year cycle of primary education due to absence of school attractiveness. There are so many reasons responsible for the alarming rate of dropout like poverty, malnutrition, absence of quality teaching-learning process in the classroom and lack of suitable learning environment at home. But the main reason behind the dropout is lack of attractions. In Bangladesh most of the primary school students come to school with a gloomy face but depart school with a smiling face due to the lack of enjoyable and child-friendly learning environment at schools.

Primary schools are generally expected to provide stimulating education for boys and girls by developing character, intellect and physical well-being within a happy scholarly and caring community. Primary schools normally play a vital part in children's lives to determine their academic, social and occupational future. These are the initial places in which children learn to face and cope with the anxieties of life. Primary schools are not only the places for learning, but also the places of possessing a positive outlook as well as developing self-esteem and self-confidence. School ambiance is also the place to develop socialization and neighborhoods within the children themselves. Therefore school climate, social and cultural environment in and outside school, safety and security within school and teachers' skill, attitude and belief are equally important and crucial for stimulating self-esteem, self-confidence and independence within children apart from ensuring academic learning. So, child friendly physical infrastructural facilities in primary schools have a pivotal role for overall development of children that enable them to make them good human beings as well as contribute generously for serving the nation in the future.

Primary schools are the schools in which children start their formal learning journey in Bangladesh and state or government run primary schools are the authentic places of mainstreaming or universalizing of primary education in the country. Since most of the primary school aged children study in the government run primary schools and significant numbers of them come from low income and poverty stricken families, vulnerable families and ethnic minority groups of peoples, therefore the government can never think of developing the country without inspiring them to become visionary. This is why primary school children remain in dire need of nourishment and more support than other students in kindergartens or private schools for developing self-confidence, commitment and self-esteem within themselves along with academic learning. Since most primary school children have fewer opportunities of enjoying better quality learning facilities at home, therefore government run primary schools should have the best quality of physical learning facilities for building them as visionary, optimistic and enthusiastic individuals by changing their attitude, outlook and belief to a great extent. Moreover government primary schools in Bangladesh should also have congenial software and hardware facilities to support a significant number of the country's primary students to get curriculum based education, personal or real education as well as ICT and vocational education to consolidate their educational and occupational future.

In Order to ensure attractive and child-friendly physical infrastructures with modern facilities, the government may construct multi storied school buildings instead of two or three separate buildings that occupy playgrounds. In the ground floor of the multi storied building there may be a hall room for multipurpose uses like celebrating occasions, conducting training/meeting, dining hall, examination hall and shelter place during natural disasters. There should be the class rooms, office rooms, library, Workshop/Laboratories for skill based learning and ICT Lab on other floors. In the ground floor there can be a room for Supportive Learning Centre (SLC), run by government selected NGOs to support underprivileged and vulnerable children (first generation learners) to dispel their learning difficulties as well as preparing daily classroom lessons at flexible time convenient to children outside school timetable. All the classrooms should be well furnished & well decorated and should have availability of natural sunlight and air. In each floor there should be toilets and wash rooms and a corner for drinking water. There should be a source of available pure water in the school. Schools should be enriched with available attractive materials for playing and teaching & learning. In each and every classroom there should be white boards/interactive white boards, push-pin boards and multimedia projector with screen. The School's physical environment should be such that children come to school with smiling faces and depart school with gloomy faces.

Discerning parents and curious children have interests in choosing schools and schools should indispensably meet the following demands of them.

Child friendly school environment

Parents always mean the effectiveness of a primary school as effectiveness of its environment as well as effectiveness in its academic results. But before selecting a primary school parents consider whether the environment of the school is child-friendly or not. To make the environment child-friendly, effective primary schools need to provide the following facilities:

Well-planned classrooms so that sufficient natural light and air easily enter the classrooms and sound from one classroom to others cannot be heard

Separate hygienic wash blocks for boys and girls with modern facilities and source of safe and pure drinking water

Adequate desks and benches for smooth sitting arrangement

Playground suitable for sports

Boundary walls so that animals and outsiders cannot enter school

Organised classrooms where whiteboard/interactive whiteboard/chalkboard is placed in a position so that writings on it can be easily visible to the students, and opportunity of hanging students' writings, drawings and other works

Digital classroom with multimedia projector, internet facility, laptop/desktop etc

Separate classroom using for Workshops or Laboratories for skill based learning

Logistic supports for keeping school premises and classrooms neat and clean with the help of teachers, student council and school brigade together

Available materials and instruments for sports and cultural activities both for boys and girls and special need students

Provision of relaxed school timetable considering season climate and socio-economic conditions of parents and school catchments areas

Academic leadership by head teacher

It is commonly said that as is the head teacher, so is the school. Therefore, the overall success of a primary school mainly depends on the leadership qualities of a head teacher. So a head teacher of an effective primary school needs to:

Act as an academic leader of a team with high vision

Work intensively with the academic and infrastructural development process of the school through involving stakeholders

Maintain an excellent rapport with students, teachers, parents and stakeholders

Monitor students' and teachers' performance regularly as an academic supervisor and provide timely feedback

Have a keen interest in organising co-curricular activities regularly to attract students to come to school and actively participate in all types of school activities

Maintain relationship with teachers like a friend

Quality teaching and learning

With a view to ensuring tangible and quality learning for all the students, teachers need to take following steps in the teaching-learning process of an effective primary school.

Come to school and attend classes timely according to class routine

Having skills of imparting lesson using digital devices

Hold classes by taking preparation of lessons at home with identifying learning outcomes and making plan for the lesson

Begin class with materials like pictures, charts etc related to lessons to make the lessons attractive to students

Incorporate individual work, pair work, group work and other interactive activities in teaching process to encourage active participation by learners

Relate lesson content to students' feelings and experience in order to involve students personally in learning

Encourage students to participate actively in the lessons by using question and answer method

Encourage students to think by asking open-ended and thought-provoking questions and help students to solve problems

Use different teaching styles and methods and adjust teaching method when needed by monitoring students' response

Monitor students' classwork and progress throughout the lesson and provide timely feedback

Identify weaker students in the lessons and take remedial measures for their learning

Display students' work that is reflective of their progress

Maintain an excellent rapport with students

Help students to use their learning in real life situation

Uses students' misconception regards to clarify their understandings to lesson

End the lesson with a review and assessing whether students' learning is achieved or not.

Mr. Khan visited lots of primary schools and observed poor quality teaching-learning activities inside classrooms in most cases. As an effective academic supervisor, he assessed unsatisfactory performances in teaching and learning by teachers and students respectively. Identifying the key reasons he took nice initiatives to talk to teachers at cluster level in presence of concerned academic supervisors with a view to improve classroom teaching.

Guidelines to improve teaching-learning process at classrooms

Teaching is a noble profession though an exhausting and demanding one. Primary school teaching or infant teaching is very challenging. Though primary teaching is a tough, stressful and unpleasant job, it is also an interesting and enjoyable profession as young children really can be the most rewarding people to work with. A primary teacher should be an inspired teacher as he/she is the architect of building the future generation of a country. Moreover, a primary teacher plays a vital role for children's social, physical, mental, moral and emotional development as he/she is directly involved with the process of their development outside the family environment. So, a primary teacher badly needs to be an inspired teacher. An inspired primary teacher is respected by all in the society as he/she demonstrates a high level of professionalism in the performance of duties not only in the teaching-learning process but also in the fields like home visit, communication with parents and involvement of parents & stakeholders with classroom activities, co-curricular and school-related activities etc. He/she values the opinion of parents and colleagues and is always eager to know and accept new ideas on teaching methods and styles to develop him/herself professionally.

Quality teaching depends on so many factors in the classroom like classroom size, teacher-student ratio, use of teaching aid and teaching methods, teachers' professional demeanor etc. But it mainly depends on the competences of the teacher on classroom management and organisation, teaching styles, resource management, assessment and progress record keeping and rapport with students. As is the teacher, so is the teaching and standard of learning of students. Therefore quality teaching by an inspired teacher helps attain equal learning by all the students in classrooms. Nowadays, primary teachers receive different types of quality training on teaching methods and techniques but the knowledge, skills and attitudes gained from training are not properly utilised in the classroom. Therefore primary education badly needs motivated teachers who will take the profession seriously as a mission, not only as a job. An inspired teacher firmly believes that only he/she can bring quality changes in the teaching-learning activities in the classroom. An enthused teacher serves with sincerity, integrity and patience in the classroom and therefore he/she contributes effectively to the teaching-learning process to make it successful. Besides performing better in the teaching-learning process in the classroom, a teacher can bring positive attitudes among the learners and parents to involve themselves in the process of infra-structural and academic development of the school.

The aim of an inspired teacher is to help all the students to attain equal learning in the classroom. Ideas of ownership and confidence are closely linked to effective teaching-learning and therefore primary teachers have a pivotal role in developing ownership and building confidence among children. With a view to ensure equal learning for all the students he/she tries to utilise the following steps to be integrated to his/her teaching-learning process:

Identifies learning outcomes and making plan for the lesson;

Enable to make digital contents for the lesson;

Makes a list of resources and the main points to be included in the lesson;

Begins class with materials like picture, chart etc related to the lessons to make them attractive to children;

Use digital devices and other materials timely;

Relates lesson content to children's feelings and experiences in order to personally involve students in learning;

Ensures children's participation in the lesson by using question and answer method;

Invites questions and encourages students to challenge concepts;

Encourages students to think by asking open-ended and thought-provoking questions;

Encourages and helps students to solve problems;

Ensures each and every child's participation by involving the class in a brainstorm, providing chances to work in a group or pair etc;

Uses different teaching styles and methods;

Closely monitors students' response to the lessons and adjust teaching method when needed as it is an established true that teachers' method is the best method in teaching;

Monitors students' class work and progress throughout the lesson and provides timely feedback;

Uses students to evaluate their homework and class work;

Assigns independent homework relevant to the lessons;

Assigns home based tasks or field work for livelihood learning and support them to complete;

Identifies weaker students and takes remedial measures for their learning;

Displays student work that is reflective of their progress

Demonstrates concern and respect for students;

Maintains an excellent rapport with students;

Helps student to build self-esteem;

Observes and monitors closely students' role, participation, behaviour and attitude to work with others and provides timely feedback;

Gives students ample opportunity to demonstrate mastery;

Helps students to use their learning in real life situation, not just storing up further knowledge and

Ends the lesson with a review and assessing students whether their learning has been achieved or not.

It is very difficult to teach primary children. It needs concentration and patience more than in other levels of the teaching profession. But primary teachers get more satisfaction and recognition from society. An inspired primary teacher is valued and respected by students, parents and all sections of people in society. Everybody salutes their contribution and dedication to perform such challenging and stressful work for building a future generation.

It is a big challenge for primary teachers to ensure each child's learning in the classrooms. Although it is challenging, it is attainable with the sincere efforts of primary teachers. Their dedication, commitment and missionary attitude would help ensure children's equal learning.

Nowadays teachers stand out in front of students and teach them the same material in the same way. Everyone is expected to do the same tasks. Some pass and some fail to do the tasks. The focus is on teaching not on learning. The teachers never think that one size does not fit all. The existing process of teaching-learning cannot ensure each and every child's learning because there are heterogeneous groups of learners in a classroom who have different socio-economic backgrounds, life experiences, interests, learning style and multiple intelligences. Learners in the primary classes also have different needs and abilities. So they do not learn the same thing in the same way in a classroom.

Considering learners' different needs, interests and abilities, a teacher can utilize the concept of differentiated learning through applying differentiated instruction in the teaching-learning process to ensure each child's learning. Primary teachers may apply the following steps:

Differentiation may begin with the creation of learning profiles for learners containing learning preferences, family backgrounds, favourite hobbies and interests.

Identify learners' level or abilities in the subject or lesson through assessing their needs and performances and use flexible grouping to group and regroup them according to their level.

Develop separate lesson plans for each learner or group of learners with similar abilities.

Assign separate tasks for each group suitable for their abilities in the same class.

Determine learners' interests. On a regular basis, ask learners to identify topics that interest them.

Assign learners different homework.

Use a variety of materials considering different learning preferences, learning styles and learning abilities.

Use a variety of activities for different groups differentiated by texts, projects, demonstration and simulation etc.

Create opportunities for learners to learn individually or in the group according to their interests.

Help learners build their own personal learning network as they can learn from their peers, other teachers and parents.

Provide a balance between teacher-assigned and learner-selected tasks to emphasise learners' choices in their learning.

It may be challenging for primary teachers to introduce differentiated instruction, as primary schools are facing problems like inadequate number of teachers and insufficient contact hours. Teachers should manage sufficient time for each class to implement differentiated instruction in the classroom. It would be better if teacher assistants are appointed at the schools to ensure each child's learning.

Mr. Khan asked his wife to share more information regarding improvement of classroom teaching as she was the then Head Teacher of a primary school. She shared her experience and emphasized developing skills of Six 'C's within students.

Once in a Grade five classroom of a Government Primary School Mrs Nahid Parvin was engaged in teaching-learning activities actively in mathematics class. Two students of the class, Sharar and Tapur, were sitting together editing each other's papers. Like them all the students in pairs were busy editing each others' papers. Ten minutes later Mrs Nahid asked them to prepare dices of geometrical objects (Square, Rectangle, Tangle, Circle etc) by using art sheets, scissors, glues, colored paper and geometry box telling them that these could be used for other classes as teaching aids. Auntika, Sadif, Lajhim, Shabab, Sudip, Tupur, Antar, Driro, Alex, Adar, Tribid Chakma, Adro, Hridoyo and other students of the class were involved actively and enthusiastically sitting in groups to complete the assignment. By the end of the stipulated time students were able to make some dice of geometrical shapes or objects. Mrs Nahid looked on with pride at the learning factory she had created in which learning took place on its own. She was also satisfied with her students' performances for creating new things. Mrs Nahid observed that the students had collaboratively created the materials and they had good and effective communication for completing the task. She noticed that in each group one boy or girl took the responsibility of giving instructions as leader of the group and other students followed him/her. Those who were not participating, other boys and girls helped them to participate. She also observed that students were able to connect achieved knowledge in geometry with the asking task to complete as an activity of application. Students criticized each other while they did wrong during the task. Sometimes they asked her without any hesitation if they faced difficulties.

The above-mentioned situation is hardly seen in the classrooms of all categories of primary school in Bangladesh. But every educator and parent must like the event to happen in the classrooms regularly. Because they want the children to not only learn skills that will help them to become good problem-solvers in academic subjects, but also to become proficient in the skills that life will require i.e. the skills of communicating, connecting, contributing, creating and collaborating. Looking a little more critically at these events in Mrs Nahid's classroom, parents and educators see children practicing the art of criticizing as a way of pursuing excellence. They also see children connecting needs, motives and ideas in ways that create potential for even more learning.

Yes, problem solving is an important educational objective. Schools should teach our children to become ever better problem-solvers. But if parents really want their children to be prepared for confidently facing the challenges of the real world, they should want development of their children's skills through practicing communicating, criticizing, connecting, creating, collaborating and contributing skills in classroom activities at schools. These are called skills of "The Six Cs"- the skills crucially needed for addressing challenges in real life situations to prepare children for the 21st century.

During closure of schools due to COVID-19, he seemed so thoughtful and observing Mr. Khan's concern his wife, Mrs. Nahid suggested that he think differently and mention following steps that may keep learners in the learning process during COVID like emergencies.

Means of continuing learning during emergencies

As learning is a continuous process, therefore by any means learning among learners should be continued amidst emergency. Before being affected by COVID, education in emergency situations might be considered during natural calamities. But the pandemic, treating also as an emergency compelled policy makers to develop innovative plans for continuing education. Closure of educational institutions due to COVID results in fatal losses in learning. The aftermath of losses in learning may become costly to keep wheels of learning rhythm into the right momentum later.

So, considering pandemic and other natural disasters as emergencies, policy makers need to chalk-out compatible and implementable plans and develop a skilled and committed workforce in the education sector for keeping students in learning all the year round. To continue students in the learning process during an emergency, front liners (teachers and education managers/administrators) need to develop professionalism. In addition, construction or renovation of infra-structural facilities, providing of emergency resilient learning friendly materials or supports, empowering front liners in developing and implanting need based plans etc are to be ensured during emergencies for continuing education.

COVID has forced an unprecedented shutdown of educational institutions and as a result huge numbers of children have been affected severely due to discontinuation of face-to-face learning. As challenges must bring some opportunities too, therefore the pandemic has provided us with an opportunity to pave the way for introducing remote learning. As the pandemic strongly demands the maintenance of social distancing rigorously, therefore there were no other alternatives to keep learners in the process of learning using multifarious platforms of remote learning. Some of the governments introduced broadcasting of digital contents of teaching-learning for primary level students through television and radio.

But impediments like absence of Internet connectivity at remote areas, non-availability of digital devices to hundreds to thousands of students of poor families, no or poor frequency of receiving lessons that has been broadcasting on TV & radio alongside with absence of TV or radio at home of poor families etc hinder to make governments' initiatives a success. Rather, introduced initiatives have been brought undesired discrimination towards ensuring inclusive learning. As introduced, remote learning methods have no access to a huge number of students; therefore some of the governments (including Bangladesh) simultaneously adopted online and offline initiatives. But success of introducing online and offline initiatives proves dissatisfactory as some teachers are found having disinterest in imparting teaching by using virtual sources. Moreover, some teachers have the apathy to visit students' homes with the assignments/worksheets (offline initiative) to support students in clarifying their understanding. A significant number of students completed or submitted home based activities with poor or no learning. Parents and guardians hardly have seen teachers encourage them to support kids to use digital devices for remote learning. But once upon a time parents witnessed primary and secondary school teachers' commitment and rapport building attitude who had the only mission of ensuring learning of students by visiting home and consulting parents. Although they didn't have the highest level of educational qualifications and training on teaching-learning, they had invisible professionalism. The pandemic reminded parents of the then teachers' professional attitude and felt a fatal absence of professionalism among nowadays teachers.

Parents and guardians have also been observing poor quality professionalism among education administrators/managers. They have been failing to motivate teachers and parents to work simultaneously for successful implementation of introduced blended methods of online and offline initiatives minimizing the challenges by utilizing existing resources. Professionalism helps administrators become proactive to motivate teachers to perform duties with missionary attitude during emergencies.

Outbreaks of the COVID-19 like pandemic may not be a one-time infectious disaster as the world community has had bitter experiences of facing immense effects of these types of outbreaks in the past. As overall development of a country mostly depends on educated and skilled workforces, therefore South Asian and African countries pivotally require keeping future generations in learning process fighting against COVID like disasters. Therefore, schools should have the practice of conducting online classes for every grade once in a week by using Google Meet/virtual platforms confirming preparation to mitigate learning losses combating against the pandemics. Regarding this, initiatives might be taken so that all students may have digital devices for ensuring access to online learning. In addition, parents may be encouraged to use smart phone/digital devices ensuring the lowest price of digital devices only for them as well as governments may consider providing smart mobile phone/Tab to students of poor families. Moreover, initiatives may be taken so that speedy Internet facilities may become available to schools and adjacent areas.

Both pandemic and other short-time emergencies demand launching of "Home and Neighbourhood Schooling". Unlike the conventional home schooling style applied in other countries, where parents or relatives or other knowledgeable persons act as instructors to conduct basic education at home, the emergency situation demanded home/neighborhood schooling may be introduced by using broadcasted lessons through television and radio as well as recorded or live teaching-learning activities from social media platforms. Lessons only on core subjects should be broadcast through radio and TV. Students might be supported by parents/relatives at home schooling and by volunteer teachers (local secondary school or college students or ex. teachers) at neighborhood schooling. Dividing primary school catchment's area proportional to number of teachers, each area may be given under a teacher to monitor and supervise home/neighborhood schooling activities and conduct face-to-face teaching once in a week to each of their concerned home/neighborhood schools. Thus students should continue the going-to-school rhythm to cope with changes caused by the pandemic and it certainly dispels monotony. But this requires launching a dedicated terrestrial education television channel by the governments. The use of mobile phone radio for receiving lessons on radio could be effective to reach students of poverty-stricken and hard-to-reach areas families. In this regard, need-based low-cost simple mobile phones with radio options might be provided to students with GO-NGO collaboration. In addition, parent/relative and volunteer teachers may provide virtual training and catchment's area based responsible teachers may facilitate virtual training.

Education in an emergency inevitably requires capacity building of teachers and education managers to develop need based emergency resilient plans and make sure of providing them monetary support along with available resources for implementation of plans.

Acknowledging remote learning- a better way for mitigating ongoing crises, the governments' initiative to broadcast lessons through television and radio is praiseworthy. But, it comes with a downside by creating inequality in terms of access to entire learners of primary education. Even children from poor and remote areas' households with lacking television and radio are deprived of receiving lessons. On the other hand, low and no tech areas students had no access to receive lessons on social platforms.

Transitioning from traditional face-to-face learning to remote learning can be an entirely different experience for the learners, which they must adapt to with little or no. Therefore, it has become essential for students to engage in offline activities and self-exploratory learning beside remote learning.

It's important to note that there is no one size fits all when it comes to learning. Policy makers need to think about for students with different needs and for students who might not have access to digital devices at low or no tech areas. So, there needs to consider following offline initiatives to be taken beside remote learning.

Weekly or fortnightly based class wise activity sheets from textbooks for core subjects might be distributed to students engaged at home/neighborhood schooling. Responsible teachers for the concerned area may collect and evaluate activity sheets weekly or fortnightly and give feedback to parent/relative and voluntary teachers to dispel students' learning weaknesses.

Voice messages might be sent to guardians' mobile numbers everyday about lesson schedules that are going to be broadcast on TV & Radio alongside following social contacting & health protocol rigorously.

Mobile phone contact with students by responsible teachers might be continued to know their interest and progress in learning alongside with providing feedback. Activities might be noted down in a registrar.

Evaluating activity sheets and considering mobile phone responses, responsible teachers need to visit supportable students home to improve their learning.

Maintaining social contact and following health rules strictly, teachers may allow students to come to school once in a week to share achievements of their students' learning and identifying ideas to be added or subtracted to existing plans.

Self-Study Learning Pack (SSLP) comprising important chapters of core subjects considering lesson plans might be developed for students. In the light of SSLP, Learning Supportive Pack (LSP) for parent/relative and voluntary teachers may be developed too. It is important to note that responsible teachers of the concerned area may support students as well as parent and volunteer teachers to use self-study materials.

Absence of good governance, intensity of committing corruption, disobeying tendency of children/youths/people to their seniors, deterioration

of morality in the society hurt Mr. Khan fatally that induced him to write national curriculum authority to introduce blended approach of both Professional Skill-based Education (PSE) and Personal, Social & Moral Education (PSME).

Proposal for developing curriculum regarding introduction of blended approach of PSE & PSME at primary and Secondary education

As education is the process of bringing desirable changes into the behavior of human beings, therefore education is not only the process of obtaining only knowledge and skills. Education is the key to ensure development, good governance and last but not the least to establish honest democracy as all of these require motivated and educated people. But the burning question is - what type of education demands? This is proved that so called educated people are responsible for committing lion parts of corruption or mega corruption in these countries. Educated bureaucrats and politicians are the main obstacle towards ensuring good governance. And influential corrupt politicians never want to change the electoral process for giving freedom to voters to choose right country friendly political leaders for honest democracy. So, a traditional knowledge based education system can never ensure development, good governance and honest democracy simultaneously. A comprehensive blended education system comprising Professional Skill-based Education (PSE) and Personal, Social and Moral Education (PSME) could be the most rational and authentic way of achieving countries' overall development by dispelling barriers towards establishing good governance and honest democracy.

PSE is a formalised approach of learning in formal educational institutions through which learners are taught content knowledge and how these are applied in real practice. The learners also acquire the necessary competencies needed for proper practice. Professional Skill-based Education (PSE) is also called career education that involves the skills learners need to be successful in job or career development. Professional education offers many-fold benefits to learners for developing their career path later.

On the other hand, Personal, Social and Moral Education (PSME) refers to helping learners acquire virtues such as honesty, responsibility and respect for others. It helps learners to learn how to live harmoniously in society. It also helps learners to live good lives and at the same time become productive and contributing members of their communities. PSME refers to helping learners to acquire a set of beliefs and a value regarding what is right and wrong. More fundamentally, it encourages learners to reflect on how they should behave and what sort of people they should be. It helps to eliminate problems like violence, dishonesty, jealousy etc from one's life.

So, the authority of National Curriculum and Textbook Board is requested to develop suitable curriculum for introducing a blended approach of education system to both PSE and PSME at primary and secondary tiers of education for the sake of ensuring country's overall development and establishment of good governance.

Mr. Khan shared the proposal for revisiting the curriculum with his wife. Mrs. Nahid suggested him to think about Livelihood Education to be included to the curriculum as it is more relevant to skill based learning

Primary Education Curriculum need to be revisited with emphasizing on Livelihood Education

Primary education curriculum in Bangladesh is one of the best. This is a competency-based curriculum developed by National Curriculum and Textbook Board (NCTB). The purpose behind starting a competency-based curriculum is to achieve learning of a combination of knowledge, skills, attitudes and values (KSAV) by learners. Competence-based curriculum stress on attaining competences by learners such as cognitive competence (knowledge gaining), functional competence (skills like thinking, doing), personal competence (knowing how to conduct oneself in a specific situation) and ethical competence (possessing personal, social and professional values). So, the focus of the competency-based curriculum is on developing learners' moral and ethical values along with knowledge and skills rather than focusing on learners' knowledge based on memorized learning from subject contents.

Young generations of the country are rushing nowadays to earn money and become rich within a very short time applying unethical or shortcut ways. They don't have any respect for their forefathers' professions such as agriculture, handicrafts etc. They seldom value people involved in informal service sectors such as street traders, rickshaw pullers, carpenters, hawkers, drivers etc and their works or professions. Their aversion, disinterest and devaluing attitude to their forefathers' livelihood professions or informal service sector professions is the sign of lacking in attaining ethical and personal competences in primary and secondary tiers of education. But the scenario was totally opposite in the past when students and even service holders took part actively in their family livelihood professions beside performing their respective duties. But young workforces need to know that still agriculture and agro based industry are the lifeline of our economy. Informal service sector is equally important to the economy for both income and employment generation as in Bangladesh about 87% of the labor force is employed in the informal sector. So, young and future generations should respect and value every profession like agriculture, fishery, livestock etc with informal service sector professions. On the other hand, due to absence of proper learning of developing values and bringing desired changes in attitude among learners, most of the educated persons are involved in committing corruption and other immoral activities nowadays.

So, this is inevitable for the government to develop competency-based curriculum in all three tiers of education so that learners can develop their morality, values and attitude along with strengthening their knowledge and skills. As the learning journey starts from elementary education, therefore primary education should get the priority to successful implementation of competency-based curriculum.

The primary education curriculum has aim, objectives, terminal competences, and grade & subject wise attainable competences. Considering subject and grade wise terminal competences, learning outcomes have been developed. Learning outcomes are the key to develop grade wise subjects or books and also subject wise contents. Therefore, the contents of books are the key to make learners capable of transferring information, knowledge, skills, attitude and values in different situations of day-to-day life. Intervention from concerned authority is essentially required to consider following initiatives to be taken regarding successful implementation of competency-based curriculum in primary education.

Grade wise number of books should become comfortable to learners. Bangla (Mother Language), English and mathematics must be the core subjects in all five classes. Considering students' interest and aptitude, one or two subjects from art & craft, music, drama and sports should be made compulsory for all grades. Beside the above mentioned core subjects, "Livelihood Education", "Religion & Moral Education" and "Elementary Science" could be the other subjects for grade three to grade five.

Contents of books and activities for learners might be developed considering all four competences to be achieved (concerned to grades) by learners. Contents and activities for learners in Bangla and English books should emphasize on grade wise learning and developing of four skills (listening, reading, writing, and speaking) of language. Keeping poems, rhymes, stories etc there might be a chapter in Bangla books for all grades (as serial) named "Amar Desh (My Country)" regards to know about country's geographical features, independence & history of emergence as a new country, historical places, affluent resources, nature, demography, religion, ethnic relations, administrative & social stratification, culture & rituals, social customs, climate, economy etc. To make it more enjoyable to students this chapter might be written as story based. Similarly, a serial chapter that introduces the world might be kept in an English book for grade three to five. This is because of discarding "Bangladesh and Global Studies" books in grade three to grade five.

Livelihood Education (LE) could be the key subject regards to make the country a developed one by 2041 along with developing learners' belief and values that every profession deserves respect because every one of those people are contributing to the society. This may be the subject for grade three to five that will present mainly elementary knowledge developing information with meager home based doable tasks with a view to make students more oriented to livelihood skills. As a skill-oriented and values developing subject, LE will not only be the source of livelihood and entrepreneurship in future but also enable students to develop love, respect and appreciation for work and workers.

There may be some broader learning areas or chapters in this book such as Family Living, Elementary Agriculture, Industrial Arts, Entrepreneurship, Basic ICT Knowledge and Occupations/Professions in Bangladesh. Contents and information might be selected or referred considering concerned grades and following "easy to little bit hard" policy. Broader learning areas may have contents selected from following topics.

Family Living: Family values and bondage, making house livable and attractive, keeping house tidy, playing with babies, rearing up older family members, maintaining good neighborhood, healthy food, keeping home and community environment clean & safe for healthy living, protecting natural & other community resources etc.

Elementary Agriculture: Vegetable & flower gardening, fruit tree growing, agricultural crops production, tea production, ducks & chicken (poultry) production, cattle production, fish production, cooperative farming, organic agriculture, food processing, uses of agro-machineries, agro-marketing etc.

Industrial Arts: Homemade food item production, production of using agro-based materials and handicrafts production (pottery, handloom, cane & bamboo craft, painting, metal craft, articles made from paper, palm leaf, cotton, cardboard etc).

Entrepreneurship: Department store & merchandising, beauty parlor, food & beverage service, salesmanship etc.

Basic ICT Knowledge: Computer hardware & software, Internet application, computer games & programs etc.

Occupations/Professions in Bangladesh: Occupations in formal sector of economy like Medical, Engineering, Teaching, ICT, Banking etc and occupations in informal sector of economy such as Carpentry & masonry, barbering, tailoring, housekeeping, tea planting & processing, plumbing, automotive servicing, electrical installation & maintenance etc.

Considering primary school as a sacrosanct place to learners and parents, the purpose of school not merely confines to impart knowledge but also to ensure holistic development of learners. So, comprehensive assessment regards to evaluate all four competences must be ensured. Students' attitude, values and behavior have never been assessed by a paper-pencil test. But without assessing attitude and values beside assessing knowledge and skills, learners' real education might not be ensured. So, "Anecdotal Notes" may be used for each and every student to assess KSAV. Teachers might be asked for compulsory use of "Anecdotal Notes" for every learner to assess their behavior, supportive attitude with classmates, rapport developing capability to students with different religion & disabilities, tendency of doing tasks together with classmates irrespective to sex & religion, mentality to support others, attitude to respect teachers & seniors, tendency of telling truth etc. In addition, home based tasks (HBT) might be given to students from grade three to five to evaluate their achievement in developing attitude and values to be respectful to people and their professions. Under HBT students may be given doable assignments such as supporting parents' to forefathers' livelihood professions or household's daily works, rearing up babies and grandfather & grandmother, gardening at roof or house premises, keeping house tidy, making homemade food, creative thinking & innovative activities etc. Reviewing "Anecdotal Note" and HBT reports, students might be brought under grading. This evaluation (grading) may be taken into account to other subjects achieved grading for final place determining grading.

During his tenure as field level education officer, Mr. Khan visited remote and disadvantaged areas where vulnerable and underprivileged people live abundantly. He witnessed a huge number of never enrolled and drop out children in these areas. Without providing equitable support to them, inclusiveness in

education can never be ensured, Mr. Khan assessed. Identifying the causes and effects of never enrolled and drop out children's contribution to economy in future, Mr. Khan stressed on GO-NGO collaboration and chalked out the following plan.

Plan for taking GO-NGO collaborative initiative for ensuring inclusiveness in basic education

Government's huge investment and intensive attention in mainstreaming of inclusive primary education has been enabling a massive success in this sector. But still the country has some remote pockets where government intervention may not be feasible to work successfully. As establishment of new schools in the pockets with few children like tea gardens, low lying areas (Haor), tribal areas, hilly areas, Chars etc is not feasible, therefore non-government agencies may come forward to create children's access to basic education. NGOs may also consider the following areas to work.

1. NGOs might be allowed to launch satellite schools up to grade two or three at above mentioned remote areas and responsible them to ensure children's mainstreaming at nearby primary school for next class enrollment

2. NGOs might be allowed to run community based "After or Before School Program (out of school)" only for students who have no or fewer learning support at home facilitated by NGO hired facilitators with the guidance of mother school teachers and concerned supervisors. This will help learners to clarify their understanding of

everyday's school lessons and prepare them for next day's lessons. Regarding this, the governments may entrust experienced NGOs with the responsibility of setting up Supportive Learning Centres (SLC) at school catchments areas. Local retired teachers or interested local unemployed educated male/female may be given the responsibility of supporting children at SLCs.
SLCs may contribute to developing reading (Mother Language & English) and numerical skills for the children as these types of learners have insufficient contact hours at primary schools and they don't have a congenial learning environment at home. There should be the provision of having a library in these centres with printed reading materials. There may be online teaching facilities so that students may get the opportunities of enjoying teaching-learning through digital contents. SLCs could take initiatives to motivate parents and guardians to make a congenial learning environment for children at home.

3. NGOs might be considered to provide support to teachers and students for ensuring timely travel to school in hard to reach haor and river belt/char areas. Regarding this, they may launch "GPS Learning Supportive Boat/Vehicle". In addition, they may launch hostel facilities for teachers & students at hilly areas.

4. Considering acute learning losses during COVID, both offline & online methods of teaching might be continued at schools. NGOs may support internet and digital device facilities to poor families' students.

5. GO-NGO collaboration may become effective for launching mid-day meal or school feeding programmes

along with supplying two sets of school dress per year and notebooks/pencils/pens for all primary school children with the financial support of donors.

5. They might be allowed to intervene for removing students' malnutrition, keeping the school environment clean & hygienic etc.

6. They may provide income generation support to poor parents of GPS students to make their learning journey smooth and hazard free.

7. NGOs might be considered for providing support to ensure effective monitoring of classroom activities by supervisory officers and taking initiatives to ensure community people & parents' active participation in school development (both academic & infrastructural) etc.

Mr. Khan witnessed that local public representatives have poor involvement and contribution to bring entire children/youths of their jurisdiction under basic education although this was one of their obligatory responsibilities. But most of them were found indifferent to implement this basic duty of ensuring each and every child/youth's hazard free access to basic education. This is because of select/elect incompetent, dishonest and untrusted public representatives. Here "Vicious cycle of illiteracy" also works to choose the right person as public representative beside weaknesses in the existing election process.

Way of electing education & people's welfare friendly public representatives

It is most ironic that voters are compelled to elect illiterate and dishonest persons as public representatives because of the existing system of election. A reason might be that mixes of honest & dishonest and friendly and non-friendly people mainly populate the pool of candidates and voters have no choice in this dimension. Making things even more complicated for voters, some candidates typically try to appear honest by mimicking honest candidates' behavior in the election campaign. Selection of good leaders depends on the quality of the candidates in the electoral race and the information available to voters alongside their development of consciousness in choosing the right person. Therefore, pre-selections of candidates as well as providing civic and voter education to voters can play a major role for bringing effective outcomes in elections.

Pre-selection system of candidates has efficacy in South Asian and African countries where a significant number of voters are economically insolvent, illiterate and politically unconscious to choose right persons as public representatives. In addition, Election Commissions (EC) also need to provide voter and civic education to voters with a view to support voters to bring leaders with honesty and trustworthy within the government and oppositions. The government and ECs may consider the following idea as innovation in election procedure.

In election, voter and civic education are necessary to ensure that all voters understand their rights and responsibilities; the contests they are being asked to decide;

what type of elections are being held; where, when and how to vote; who the candidates are; values of their verdict; value of democracy and importance of their selection. ECs need to take adequate and effective initiatives to provide voter and civic education to voters. Initiatives such as organization of awareness meetings at villages/slums; broadcast motivational documentaries on Radio, TV, local dish channels and social media; arranging awareness building shows of popular theatre/street drama/folk song etc may take to educate voters.

Poverty is the premier hurdle towards ensuring inclusive education. This is also the crucial reason for providing the same qualitative learning to entire primary school children. Poverty is responsible for irregular attendance of students at school, leaving school without completing the primary cycle, non-attentive participation in classroom activities and never enrolled at school. Mr. Khan knows that skill-based or work based learning is the key to ensure involvement of poverty-stricken families' children into jobs after completion of learning. Realizing the importance of poverty alleviation on ensuring smooth access to basic education as well as ensuring quality learning of vulnerable families' children he therefore presented a proposal to the authority regards to address the vital issue.

Proposal for inaugurating skill or work based education for children of underprivileged families

Children that are out of school tend to be mostly from economically disadvantaged households and vulnerable populations of urban slums and hard to reach/remote areas like low-lying marsh lands, tea gardens, tribe inhabited areas, hilly areas etc. Above mentioned areas' vulnerable families also have financial problems that certainly discourage them from receiving the basic education of their children. So, they need to provide not only the opportunities of acquiring foundational literacy and numeracy but also to provide skill-developing training to make them employable and competent or to the labour market.

Work-based learning can provide a strong learning environment and develop job oriented skills to out of school children. Employers must get benefit by recruiting these learners through utilizing productive skills of them. The country also benefited from an increase in skilled labour and ensuring out of school children's smoother transition from school to stable employment without heavy government investment.

Work-based learning is a promising way of engaging never enrolled or dropped out youths to work by making them employable through providing skills development training as well as foundational literacy and numeracy knowledge. Work-based learning provides young people with an alternative way to learn that is a blend of job-oriented and academic. It can provide a bridge into careers, equip them with skills that are in demand in the labour market and connect them to potential employers.

Employers or industry owners' engagement is essential to make work-based learning initiatives for out of school children/youths a success. Therefore, finding ways to make work-based learning more attractive to employers is a key challenge for policy makers. The governments need to motivate employers by clarifying the philosophy of this philanthropic initiative that it not only provides an opportunity for employers to show social responsibility, but also be well aligned with their business objectives. There may be an MOU with the governments and employers for providing logistic and monetary support to run the work-based learning centres as a collaborative initiative. Learners also have a contract with the concerned employers to work for the employers for a stipulated time with the rationale wages.

Work-based learning may promote and develop both academic and skill development, learning of out-of school children and empowering them to become successful in the job market. Their developed job-oriented skills and achieved academic knowledge may be demanded by the international labour market too. Therefore, developing a significant number of out of school children into skilled workforces by nourishing them through launching work-based learning centres should get the most priority to the governments and the following step might be considered by the governments.

The governments may sign an MOU to the employers to run countrywide work-based learning centres providing logistic, technical and monetary support. Curriculum development and management related activities might be administered by the concerned ministry and directorate.

Authorities for exporting manpower may be given responsibility of running skill development centres at district level so that skilled manpower might be developed for international labour market recruitment.

Skill development training courses might be selected considering the learning centre area's labour market demand as well as local natural resources that have alignment to used raw materials by the employers. Target students' family profession may also be considered regarding selection of training courses.

Flexible timetables comfortable to learners may become effective for smooth running of the centres. In addition, the students might be provided nutritious food and a monthly stipend.

www.ingramcontent.com/pod-product-compliance
Lightning Source LLC
LaVergne TN
LVHW050425160726
843469LV00041B/1237